Sally was born and brought up in Bath, Somerset. She showed a talent for creative writing at an early age with short stories for school assignment and discovered a particular talent for writing poetry in her teenage years. She incorporates her passion of horse riding, running and the outdoors in her poetry.

Sally is divorced and now lives with new boyfriend and his children. She has two ex-race horses and two dogs and continues to pursue her passion in racing.

I would like to dedicate this book to my boyfriend, Paul, who has supported me; to my best friend, Becky, who was always there for me and to my English teacher, Mrs Rodgers, who recognised my ability at school and encouraged me to continue to write.

Sally R. Giles

DIVERSITY

AUSTIN MACAULEY PUBLISHERS™

LONDON • CAMBRIDGE • NEW YORK • SHARJAH

A CIP catalogue record for this title is available from the British Library.

ISBN 9781398405417 (Paperback)
ISBN 9781398405424 (ePub e-book)

www.austinmacauley.com

First Published (2021)
Austin Macauley Publishers Ltd
25 Canada Square
Canary Wharf
London
E14 5LQ

This book would not have been presented for publication if it wasn't for the following people:

My ex-husband shown for recognising and encouraging my talent.

My boyfriend Paul for all his help and support.

My family for their support.

My awesome editors and their team for recognising my talent and working with me to publish it.

Stuck

This silence is golden, this silence is key
To let my heart tell me what matters to me.
Noise and distractions, disruptions and such
Are just an elusion that matter not much.
I need silence to hear and silence to see
The lights and sounds which are all around me.
I need to be able to see into my soul
So I can work out what's wrong and make it my goal
To let myself recover, allow me to heal
My mind, body and soul which are broken.

I'm broken through years of being someone I'm not,
Broken in ways in which I know not what
I am anymore, or who I once was,
Where am I hiding and how do I find
My spirit, my spark, curiosity and mind?
I am lost, I am broken, I'm losing my head
I'm surrounded in darkness, how do I tread
My way back to a healthy, happy young soul?

I'm stuck in a shell like a crab in the sea,
How do I find my way back to me?
I need to find light, I need to find trees,

Breathe in the scent of a newly cut breeze.
I need to hear silence, I need time to heal,
I need time to gather my thoughts and to feel
Like I'm someone again with a purpose.

Nothing in This Life Is Bad

Look at me and dry your tears,
Hide away your hurts and fears.
There is nothing I can do
Except to watch and comfort you.
Try to tell me what is wrong,
You can't go on like this for long.
You can't go on and live this life
With too much worry, hurt and strife.
Come here, sit down and talk to me,
Dry your tears and you shall see
That nothing in this life is bad,
So wipe your eyes and don't be sad.

Dancing in the Breeze

I'm a little fairy dancing in the breeze,
I'm a little fairy swinging through the trees,
I'm a little fairy dancing high
Staring at the great blue, darkening sky.

I'm a little fairy dancing in the breeze,
I'm a little fairy sitting in the leaves,
I'm a little fairy bright and true,
I'll come to you and help you through.

Memories

The trees blow softly in the breeze,
Dust swirls up around me.
I see your liquid, soft brown eyes,
I feel your love surround me.

The sun is shining on your face,
It makes your soft coat shine.
I watch your fine exquisite grace
As you walk, I'm glad you're mine.

Your kiss and touch are so sublime,
They give me a new dimension.
Your love and mine are so combined,
I feel your adoration.

The blowing wind, it dries my tears,
I miss you now that you're gone,
The memories I keep locked inside
Will be with me for ever more.

My heart is breaking, I want you so,
I wish that you were here.
The anguish, tears and love won't go,
But your presence is always near.

The Storm

The sound of the wind, the wetness of rain,
The waves splashing in again and again.
I'm trying to run but my breath comes too fast,
The day is so dark, will it be my last?

The sand clings to my frozen feet,
The crashing waves, they match the beat
Of my heart, it's squeezed and taught with fright,
But you come to me on this stormy night.

Rain drips steadily from my hair,
Why did you come to me? Why did you dare
To run out in this stormy night
Just to see that I am alright?

Look Out the Window

Look out the window, open your eyes,
Look at the world, don't say goodbye.
Look out the window, watch as the trees
Bend and blow in the summer breeze.

Look out the window, think about you,
Think of the people who love you too.
Look out the window, think about them,
They all want to see you again.

Look out the window, what can you see?
A bird, a plane, a furry striped bee?
Look out the window, watch the trees blow,
And know that no one wants you to go.

I Will Wait

My chest is constricted, my throat is dry,
My eyes are sore but I will not cry.
I stare unseeing at a newly dug grave,
You're silently begging me to be brave,
Because there's no release from my pain and sorrow
But I will shed my tears tomorrow.
Although my grief won't go away,
I will wait to weep another day.
I'm fighting back the tears that threaten
To fall, but then I am forgetting
That although there's no release from sorrow,
I will wait to shed my tears tomorrow.

The Dark

The darkness spits out wind and rain,
As I walk, I stumble now and again,
The fog draws in, the rain increases,
As I stumble along, the darkness reaches
To enfold me in its shadowy depths.

I'm trying to walk in a big black hole,
Claustrophobia seeps in and takes a hold.
My breath comes faster, panic sinks in,
My heart is stuttering, then a cold wet thing
Reaches out to touch my shoulder.

I whip around and scream in fear,
It was just a branch I passed too near,
Oh how I hate this dark wet night
With so many things to cause me fright
Lurking in the blackness.

It's dark and cold, there's wind and rain,
As I walk, I stumble, once again,
Then a light appears not far away
Now I know I'll find a way
To reach my house in safety.

A Single Rose

One single rose, one little kiss,
That's all it took, now how I miss
The long dark evenings on our own,
But now you're gone and I'm alone.

The wind is shuddering through the air,
I feel your fingers in my hair,
Trees are blowing, the moon comes out,
I know you're there, without a doubt.

I feel your penetrating gaze,
Those eyes that made my spirits ablaze,
Then I realise that I am dreaming
And just how thoughtless I am being.

You were here, now you've gone again,
Give me something to break the pain,
You loved me but you had to part,
Please know you'll always be in my heart.

Phobia of the Dark

Twilight fades across the sky,
Making the daylight say goodbye.
Once twilight starts, the night settles in
And then the dark thoughts all begin.

Horror hits me as the night grows darker
And the atmosphere becomes much quieter,
I'm caught out in the dark alone,
Panic picks up, ramming it home.

Panic hits hard, like a sudden pain,
Then quite suddenly it begins to rain.
My feet take off, my body follows,
I'm breathing fast, I cannot swallow.

A scary shadow, it's just a tree,
But I hear footsteps keeping pace with me.
The rain pours down, my feet gather speed
To get me away as fast as I need.

Dream On

Close your eyes and shut your mind,
Let the world wash over you, give yourself time
To fade away from the mountain of noise,
So close your mind and dream on deep.

When you're feeling down and misunderstood,
Just take a deep breath and maybe you should
Slip away to the land of dreams,
So shut your mind and dream on deep.

No need to wait for the dark to appear,
Just close your mind and maybe you'll hear
Ghostly hoof beats, the crashing of waves,
So wherever you are, just dream on deep.

Twilight Image

Your face is etched before my eyes,
Your image never really dies,
I see your eyes, your long fair hair,
Oh why did you go? It isn't fair.

Your image now, it makes me cry,
Did you really have to die?
I think of the things we used to do
Before you died, it was just us two.

Your face begins to slowly fade,
As darkness steps towards your grave,
It's getting cold, I'm shivering here,
Oh please come back, I need you near.

Crossroads

I'm walking through a hazy mist,
I'm walking without you.
I need your constitution here
To tell me what to do.

I've reached a crossroad in my life,
I need you by my side.
The mist is growing thicker now,
You need to be my guide.

The mist has gone, replaced by fear,
You're far away from me.
The fear has cruelly stolen sight
From me, I cannot see.

I'm standing in a dead-end dream,
What's happening is not true.
This dream cannot be real, but hey
It is and I'm missing you.

Fear

Rain and thunder crashing down
From the cloudy skies.
Trees and objects blowing round,
Who can hear my cries?

It's dark and cold out here tonight,
I'm trying to find my way.
It's becoming terribly hard to fight
My fear, it's mounting high.

The weather out here becomes so strong,
My steps have gone astray.
Where's your hand to guide me back?
To send me on my way?

Broken Heart

Tears from your eyes fall steadily down,
Why do you always weep and frown?
Is it because someone was taken from you?
And you can't think of what to do?
I will come and dry your tears,
Whisper away your hurts and fears.
You can come and join in with me
Or are you afraid that I will be
Taken away and we'd have to part?
I know you don't want that, it'll break your heart.

Wild and Free

I really want to be outside,
Where there my dignity and pride
Can never be taken away from me,
Out there I will be wild and free.

In the forest, in the trees,
Sitting among the deep green leaves,
Pondering how it is to be
In the forest, wild and free.

Never again will I go inside,
Into the classroom where my pride
Will be taken again from me,
I'm proud of being wild and free.

Wild and free, free and wild,
Leaping and frolicking like a child,
Dancing in the bright, fresh air
With the breeze rustling my golden hair.

The Cry I Heard in the Night

The cry I heard in the night
Was really heart-breaking.
My soul went dead with fright.
I knew it was you when I woke.
Live with me now
Or I will surely die.
Don't walk away from me,
Don't leave me alone,
We all heard your cry.

A world heard your cry,
What's the matter?
Are you going to tell me?
A world heard your cry.
Your cry woke me from my sleep,
A scream full of anguish.
If you go, I'll die friendless,
All the hope in the world will be gone.
You have to stay for me,
Don't walk away from me,
Don't leave me alone,
We all heard your cry.

My Days Are Empty

The darkness slowly fades away,
Dawn comes with a bright red sky,
Another sleepless night I've had,
Another painful vision of you,
Please come back to me.

My days are empty without you,
The sky doesn't ever seem to be blue.
My days are empty without you,
The sky is always damp and grey,
I need you to fulfil my day.

My days are empty, dark and dank,
My vision is cloudy, my mind is blank.
Outside it begins to slowly rain,
I can't get rid of all this pain.
Please come back to me,
My days are empty without you.

Spring Time

It's spring time now, the flowers are out,
The lambs are born, they frisk about,
The sun is shining, the grass is green,
The stream is flowing so very clean.

The meadow grass is lush and long,
The winter crispness is long gone,
The sun is shining, birds are gay,
As they fly high on this beautiful day.

This World Full of Light

The sun goes down, shining bright,
It seems the world is full of light,
The sky shines brightly, crimson red
As I lay down my weary head.

The sky looks like it is on fire,
From outside I can hear the choir
Of trees swaying gently back and forth,
Cascading to me from the north.

My Little Lenny

The summer breeze stirs up your mane,
You toss your head so proudly.
I see your white star shining bright,
I hear your neigh sound loudly.

You canter quickly to the gate,
You're the first one there.
Your ears are pricked, your eyes alert,
As you wait for me so fair.

You're always there when I arrive,
You greet me with a whinny.
I stroke your nose, so smooth and soft,
You're mine, my little Lenny.

The bond we have, the trust we share
Has taken us so far.
You're my chestnut man with a golden mane
And a shining star.

I miss your ears, your eyes, your face,
Your shining chestnut coat.
I miss your loving, warm embrace,
Your soft and whiskery nose.

You've always been mine, my little man,
We've always been together.
I'll never forget you, I love you so,
You'll be in my heart forever.

Look in My Eyes

Look in my eyes and you will see
Everything that you mean to me.
Beyond the surface, through the wall
Of protection, guarding, you'll see it all.

I come across as cold and fierce,
My layers of armour you must pierce.
If you search my heart and my soul,
You'll find secrets hidden, never told.

Look in my eyes and you will see
The strength and power I can be,
Look in my eyes and you'll find trust
That together this nightmare we will bust.

The Quarry Accident

I open my eyes to a world of pain
And fear, I don't know where I am.
I'm in the open, the air is chilly,
I'm lying on something rocky and hard.

Panic engulfs me, where am I?
What has happened? Why do I hurt?
Why am I lying on a pile of rocks?
Fear mounts high, then I remember.

I'm in the quarry, I fell off the edge,
Forty-foot drop onto the rocks below.
Common sense takes over, I need to move,
Stop being weak, get up and walk.

My body is broken, I cannot walk,
I have a concussion, I'm dizzy and sick.
I'm cold, I'm shaking, I'm very scared
As I collapse once again to the ground.

All night I lie in the quarry alone
In pain and fear, shaking with cold.
I wonder if anyone knows that I'm here
And will come to rescue me.

Anorexia

I'm trapped inside this prison cell,
I can't escape, I've tried.
I'm stuck inside a nightmare, tell
Me what to do, I'm tired.

I'm tired, exhausted of fighting you,
This voice that won't be still.
You live inside my head, you know
You're in control of me.

You speak to me all day and night,
You're loudest when I'm quiet.
Tormenting me, you're always right,
You know I'll lose the fight.

I've tried to fight you once or twice,
I've fought so hard, it's true,
But every time I've paid the price,
I'll never be free of you.

The Elements

In the cold, the wind and rain,
I stand and lift my face to claim
The feeling of peace, refreshment and calm
That I only feel when the wind blows.

I feel its fingers touch my face
And spread a calm across myself.
It lifts my hair and stings my eyes
But a feeling of peace resides in me.

I love the wind, it calms me so
When it blows across the miles.
I love the clean fresh air it brings
Along with the refreshing rain.

Out here in the elements I'm wild and free,
Out here I feel I can truly be me,
I love the cold, the wind, the rain,
This feeling of peace that brings no pain.

Over the Edge

Who hears my cries out in the wild?
I'm calling, crying like a child.
I'm running, stumbling over treacherous ground
Wondering if I will be found.
I've been out here all night alone
Wishing I was safely home.
I'm shouting, calling into the dark,
I'm tripping, cursing, my feet won't work.
I'm falling, tumbling through the air,
I went over the edge but how? And where
Am I going to land? Will I even survive
A fall from this height? Will I still be alive?
When I hit the ground, it's going to hurt,
I tense myself to embrace the dirt.
I remember nothing, no impact, no pain,
But when I wake up, nothing is ever the same.

The Chestnut Stallion

I stand at the gate and click my tongue,
He'll raise his head and then he'll come
Cantering through the old dead grass,
I wonder how he comes to pass
His time in this lonely field.

He slithers to a stop in front of me,
He's waiting impatiently to see
What I have brought for him to eat,
Something tasty? Something sweet?
To brighten his long dark day.

He pushes forward his chestnut head,
Eagerly waiting as I have said
For the tasty morsel in my hand.
He already knows it's something grand,
Because he gets it every day.

As he chews I stroke his nose,
And he doesn't mind because he knows
That I won't hurt him, I'm his friend.
In his haste for more, he bends
The wire that pens him in.

He is a stallion he needs to be
In the country wild and free.
He is a stallion, he needs to breed,
He needs to he needs to gallop, drink and feed,
I wish I could set him free.

The Wrong Road

I walked the wrong road once again,
A road full of tears, fear and pain.
All for a dream, all for you,
But you were just leading me on.

I wake up with the moon in my face,
The warmth of your body is long gone,
You were magic, a dream come true,
But you were just leading me on.

I've walked this road many times before
A road full of sorrow, anger, regret
A road of loss, a road of pain
A road I'll never walk again.

I'll never feel your fiery kiss
You'll always be the one I miss
I'll never touch, feel your skin
Because you were just leading me on.

The Sea

Atop a cliff, staring down
Into the eyes of the sea,
Watching the waves as they crash around
And fling themselves at me.

I stare into the fathomless eyes,
I watch the spray fly up,
I feel at peace, I'm quite relaxed,
It is here that I feel free.

The waves now crumble into shore,
They break upon the shingle,
The current claims them back once more,
The waves and pebbles mingle.

Daydreaming

My eyes grow distant, I've left the room,
I hate this building, this place, this room.
I yearn to be outside, not here,
This room, this place, I'll always fear.

I hate to be locked up inside,
In this room I cannot hide.
Away from prying eyes and smirks,
Inside this room my hatred lurks.

My eyes grown distant, I've left the room
This ever-present fear and gloom
I leave behind the searching eyes
Out here my tempered spirit flies.

My Positive Touch

To me you are my positive touch,
I lean on you, you're like a crutch.
The wind it blows your coal black hair,
You move like a shadow through the air.

I need you in my life so much
Because you are my positive touch.
Your strength, your poise, your lightning speed
Are all that I ever truly need.

Please don't ever abandon me,
I need you near, I want to see
Your love for me shine in your eyes,
This special love will never die.

Change

Change is necessary, change is good
Everyone says, but maybe they should
Take time to think about what they mean
Because after change nothing stays the same.

It's tumultuous, stressful and full of strife,
But apparently change is part of life.
It's difficult to cope, hard to think,
But we just have to hold our heads high.

With change a lot of people thrive,
Thoughts of positivity, drive
Are present in their heads, spurring them on.
For me change is worse than a bomb.

Nightmare

His hand pressing down upon your mouth
You haven't time to scream or shout.
His weight is on you weighing you down,
Your hands and feet are tightly bound.
You struggle and fight, to no avail,
You wriggle, squirm, but he's far too strong.
His weight it crushes you painfully,
Stop fighting in the hope that he
Won't hurt or cause you any more pain.
Your body aches and once again
You wonder how he managed to creep
Into your room, where you asleep.
How thoughtless to let your eyelids close
And encourage the nightmare to impose
Upon your mind, it will always come
When you're asleep and no one's home
To hear your screams and save you.

Galloping Free

I feel the wind, it stings my face,
I hear the pounding hooves,
I feel the power, the restless pace,
The way his body moves.

I feel the power, speed and grace,
Beneath me moving fast,
My hands on his neck, his lengthening gait,
He refuses to be last.

I feel his sweat, slick on his neck,
His muscles bunch and lengthen,
He stumbles, will we hit the deck?
He recovers, his stride it strengthens.

I adore this speed, the way he runs,
The sweat upon him gleams.
His hooves pound the ground, he's having fun,
Together we are a team.

Falling

It's unbelievable how, if you think about this,
I went hurtling down into an empty abyss
Past jagged rocks and flimsy trees,
It seemed to last for an eternity.

It felt as if I was in the air
Forever, the wind was whipping my hair,
A feeling of calm passed through my body,
I had to just leave my fate to gravity.

I don't recall landing or feeling at all
Frightened, I just knew I needed to crawl
Away from this hole, but my body was broken,
I was out here alone, in the big empty open.

I couldn't crawl far, I was too weak and in pain,
But I wouldn't give up and time and again.
I dragged myself across the stony ground
To somewhere I thought I may be found.

All night I lay there, crawling and resting
In a fog of pain, concussion and guessing
When I'd be found, would my dogs go for help?
They stayed by my side, wouldn't leave me alone.

Exhausted, broken and very near death,
The next morning help came, I had no breath
To explain what had happened, I lay in a mist
Of pain, confusion and relief at a near miss
That I had had with death.